The Life and Work of... Pieter Bruegel

Jayne Woodhouse

Heinemann Library
Chicago, Illinois

Customer Service 1-888-454-2279

Visit our website at www.heinemannlibrary.com

Designed by Celia Floyd
Illustrations by Karin Littlewood, Illustrators co.
Originated by Dot Gradations
Printed in Hong Kong/China

05 04 03 02
10 9 8 7 6 5 4 3 2 1

Library of Congress Cataloging-in-Publication Data
Woodhouse, Jayne, 1952-
      Pieter Bruegel / Jayne Woodhouse.
          p. cm. – (The Life and work of--)
      Includes bibliographical references and index.
      Summary: Briefly examines the life and work of the sixteenth-century Flemish painter, describing and giving examples of his art.
      ISBN 1-57572-344-1 (lib. bdg.)   ISBN 1-4034-0500-X (pbk. bdg.)
      1. Bruegel, Pieter, ca 1525-1569—Juvenile literature. 2.
Painters—Belgium—Biography—Juvenile literature. [1. Bruegel, Pieter, ca. 1525-1569. 2.
Artists. 3. Painting, Flemish. 4. Art appreciation.] I. Title. II. Series.

ND673.B73 W66 2000
760'.092—dc21
[B]   00-025791

Acknowledgments
The Publishers would like to thank the following for permission to reproduce photographs:

Bridgeman Art Library, pp. 5, 21; The Stapleton Collection, p. 4; Alan Jacobs Gallery, London, p. 6; Kunsthistorisches Museum, Vienna, pp. 7, 11, 13, 23, 25; Museum voor Schone Kunsten, Ghent, p. 16; Musées Royaux des Beaux-Arts de Belgique, Brussels, pp. 17, 19; Johnny van Haeften Gallery, London, p. 18; Hessisches Landesmuseum, Darmstadt, p. 27; British Museum, pp. 9, 15; C. H. Bastin and J Evrard, p. 26; Heinemann, p. 29; Robert Harding Picture Library/Adam Woolfitt, p. 10

Cover photograph reproduced with permission of ET Archive

Every effort has been made to contact copyright holders of any material reproduced in this book. Any omissions will be rectified in subsequent printings if notice is given to the Publisher.

Some words in this book are in bold, **like this.** You can find out what they mean by looking in the glossary.

Contents

Who Was Pieter Bruegel?

Pieter Bruegel lived nearly 500 years ago. He is one of the greatest artists to come from the **Netherlands.** This **portrait** of Pieter was made in 1572.

Pieter is famous for his paintings of everyday life. They show how ordinary people lived a long time ago. Pieter did this painting of **peasants** dancing in 1568.

Early Life

We know very little about Pieter's early life. He was probably born in Breda, a town in the **Netherlands.** It was around 1525.

Pieter left no writings. Most of our information about him comes from his pictures. He may have included a picture of himself in this painting. Look on the right-hand edge.

Becoming an Artist

Pieter learned to paint in Antwerp, a town in Belgium. His teacher was an artist named Pieter Coecke van Aelst. When Pieter was about 26, he opened his own **studio**.

Pieter lived in Antwerp for about twelve years. Antwerp was a rich and important town. Pieter did his first paintings there. Here is one of his early paintings.

Foreign Travels

Soon after he became an artist, Pieter traveled for three years. First, he went to Italy. In Rome, he saw the Colosseum, a famous **monument**.

Pieter remembered the places he had seen. Sometimes he painted these places in his artwork. Look at his painting below. The large building in the center looks like the Colosseum.

Sketches

On his way home from Italy, Pieter traveled through Switzerland. He made many drawings of the mountains he saw there.

About ten years later, Pieter painted this
winter **scene**. Pieter painted the Swiss
mountains he remembered in the background.

Drawings

Pieter returned home to Antwerp in 1555. He went to work for Hieronymus Cock, a well-known **printmaker**. Hieronymus made **engravings** from Pieter's drawings.

Here is an engraving of Pieter's drawing. Pieter did this engraving himself. In Pieter's time, an engraving was a way to make copies of a picture.

Paintings

Some of Pieter's paintings are in the **style** of Hieronymus Bosch. Bosch was a very popular artist. His pictures were full of strange people, as you can see in this picture of Christ with his cross.

This is part of one of Pieter's paintings. You can see how he has used Bosch's ideas.

Marriage

In 1563, Pieter married Mayken Coecke van Aelst. She was the daughter of his old teacher. They went to live in Brussels. This is what Brussels looked like then.

Pieter worked very hard. In the next six years, he finished thirty of his most famous paintings. These were done in Pieter's own **style**. This one was painted in 1566.

The Seasons

In 1565, a rich **merchant** asked Pieter to paint some pictures. The pictures would decorate the merchant's house.

Pieter painted six **scenes**. They show the changing seasons. This picture shows summer. The one on page 13 shows winter. Only five of the paintings can still be seen. The sixth one has been lost.

21

Ordinary Lives

Most artists in Pieter's time only painted rich and important people. But Pieter wanted to show how ordinary people lived. He watched people at events like this wedding.

Many of Pieter's paintings are about **peasant** life.
Some of his paintings are like puzzles. Here, the
bride is at the center of the table. But which figure
is her husband?

Children's Games

In Pieter's time, there were no newspapers or television. People looked at pictures for entertainment and to learn about things.

In this picture, Pieter drew more than 80 different games. You might recognize some of the games children liked to play. Children still play them today.

A Family of Artists

Pieter's sons, Pieter and Jan, became artists. So did his grandsons. But Peter died in 1569, when his children were still young. He is buried in this church in Brussels, Belgium.

This is one of Pieter's last paintings. It is called *The Magpie on the Gallows.* It was finished the year before he died.

Lost and Found

For a long time, people forgot about Pieter. They no longer liked his **style** of painting. Many of his pictures were lost or destroyed.

Then, about 100 years ago, people began to look at Pieter's work again. They realized that his paintings were really **masterpieces**. Today, Pieter is a very popular artist.

Timeline

1525–30   Pieter Bruegel probably born around this time in Breda, Netherlands—exact date and place of birth unknown

1540s   Trains with Pieter Coecke van Aelst

1551   Becomes a Master of the Painters' Guild in Antwerp

1551–4   Travels to Italy and Switzerland

1554   Works for **printmaker** Hieronymus Cock in Antwerp

1557–69   Pieter paints the 40 paintings for which he is best known

1563   Marries Mayken Coecke van Aelst and moves to Brussels

1564   Pieter and Mayken's first son, Pieter, born

1565   Paints *The Seasons* for a **merchant** named Nicolaas Jonghelinck

1568   Pieter's son Jan is born

1569   Pieter dies and is buried at Notre-Dame de la Chapelle, Brussels

Glossary

engraving   picture cut into a metal plate, covered with ink, and then pressed onto paper

masterpiece great work of art

merchant   person who buys and sells goods

monument   ancient building or building meant to honor someone

Netherlands country in western Europe now sometimes called Holland

peasant   man or woman who lives and works on land owned by someone else, such as a king

portrait   painting of a person

printmaker   person who makes copies of a drawing or painting

scene place where something happens

studio   room or building where an artist works

style   particular way an artist shows ideas in his or her work

---

More Books to Read
An older reader can help you with these books.

Malam, John. *Pieter Breugel.* Minneapolis, Minn.: Lerner Publishing Group, 1999.

Muhlberger, Richard. *What Makes a Bruegel a Bruegel?* New York: Penguin Putnam Books for Young Readers, 1993.

More Paintings to See
Noah's Ark, The Getty Museum, Los Angeles, California

The Harvesters, Metropolitan Museum of Art, New York, New York

The Three Soldiers, The Frick Collection, New York, New York

The Rabbit Hunters, National Gallery of Art, Washington, D.C.

Index